Instructional Fair's *Decimals and Percents — Grade 6* is just one of a series of Basic Skills books that can be used by parents, teachers or tutors to help students master essential skills taught in the sixth grade.

This book is designed both to instruct students and to provide them with practice in decimal and percent concepts taught in the sixth grade. Each skill/concept is presented on two pages. The first page includes step-by-step instructions and guided practice. This does not take away the need for instruction of the skill, but rather reviews the skill taught, enabling the student to work independently with examples to follow. The guided practice serves to reinforce the skill/concept before students go on to the second page. The second page features a fun type of activity and allows for independent practice. These activity pages have many formats including crossword puzzles, mazes and decoding messages. They are designed to let students have fun as they practice new mathematical skills.

Ideally, the skills/concepts presented in this book will be taught in the classroom or at home using manipulatives. Students will be better able to grasp the material with the use of concrete objects, especially if they have problems with a particular skill.

Besides teachers, tutors and parents will also find this book useful. The instructional page can be done along with the student, and the fun practice page will show that not all math homework has to be dry and boring. Some of it can actually be enjoyable!

This book covers 21 sixth grade decimal and percent concepts. The answers to the activities can be found on pages 44-48. Other books with this same format for sixth grade that you might wish to consider include *Fractions* and *Math Topics*.

Decimal Place Value

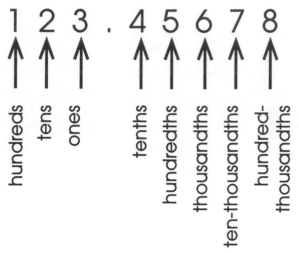

.049__8__ has 8 ten-thousandths

2.1__3__76 has 3 hundredths

.__4__58 has 4 tenths

.1__9__2 has 9 hundredths

4.6012__5__ has 5 hundred-thousandths

1. The number 24.56137 has:

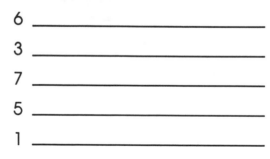

6 _____

3 _____

7 _____

5 _____

1 _____

2. What number has:

4 hundredths

0 tenths

3 ten-thousandths

5 hundred-thousandths

8 thousandths

_____

Profound Pork

What do you call a smart pig? To find out, write the word name for each underlined number. When you are done, read the circled letters from top to bottom.

67.071<u>4</u> = __ __ __ ◯ __ — __ __

14.5<u>6</u>9 = __ __ ◯ __ —

.2080<u>1</u> = __ __ __ ◯ __ —

.3<u>4</u>7 = __ ◯ __ — __

3.511<u>2</u> = __ __ ◯ __ —

63.<u>8</u>5 = __ ◯ __ —

2.40<u>5</u> = __ __ ◯ __ —

8.1<u>7</u>04 = __ __ ◯ __ —

3

Comparing and Ordering Decimals

Compare: 14.0397, 14.0386

To compare decimals, line up decimal points and compare each place value starting from the left until they differ.

same →

14 . 03	97
14 . 03	86

← different

Since 9 is greater than 8, 14.0397 > 14.0386.

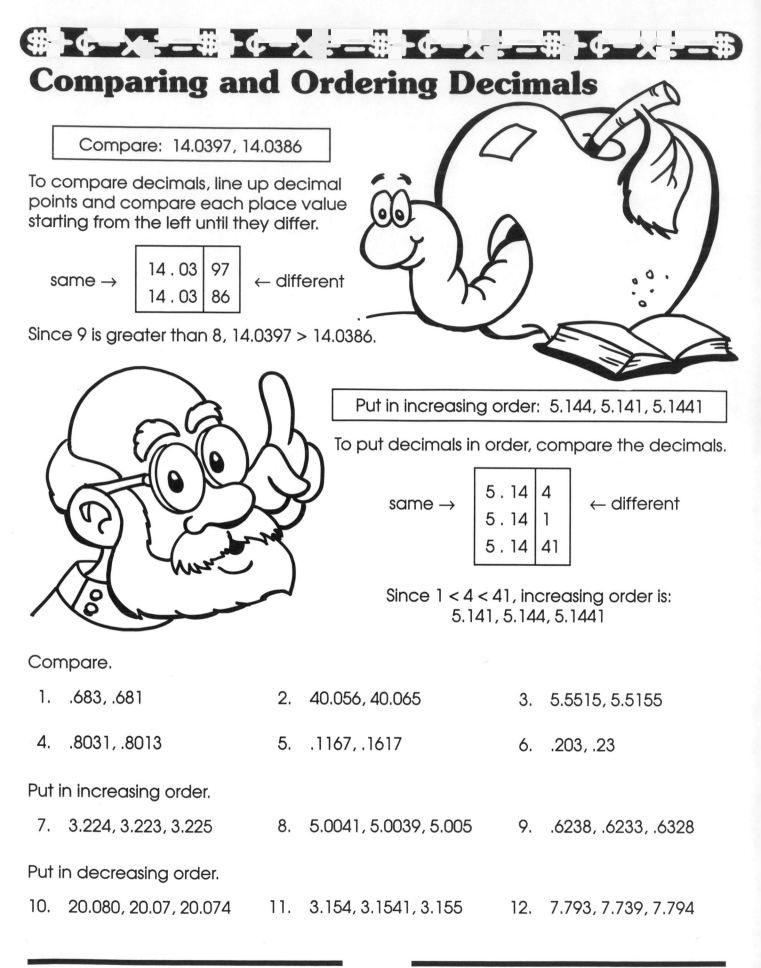

Put in increasing order: 5.144, 5.141, 5.1441

To put decimals in order, compare the decimals.

same →

5 . 14	4
5 . 14	1
5 . 14	41

← different

Since 1 < 4 < 41, increasing order is:
5.141, 5.144, 5.1441

Compare.

1. .683, .681

2. 40.056, 40.065

3. 5.5515, 5.5155

4. .8031, .8013

5. .1167, .1617

6. .203, .23

Put in increasing order.

7. 3.224, 3.223, 3.225

8. 5.0041, 5.0039, 5.005

9. .6238, .6233, .6328

Put in decreasing order.

10. 20.080, 20.07, 20.074

11. 3.154, 3.1541, 3.155

12. 7.793, 7.739, 7.794

Marvelous Mentor!

What is another word for teacher? To find out, solve problems 1-9. Then, find the answers in the chalkboard and put the corresponding letter above that question's number. Then, solve the rest of the problems.

O = .0111	U = 17.666	G = 8.04	B = 31.039
U = 6.499	P = .1368	A = 5.614	I = 5.6
T = 26.892	E = 26.98	G = 12.82	E = 17.675
M = .1376	L = 8.043	U = .0049	D = 31.0299

Which decimal is largest?

1. 5.614, 5.6114, 5.6

2. 26.892, 26.98

3. .0049, .0005, .0111

4. 17.675, 17.666

Which decimal is smallest?

5. 8.043, 8.04

6. 31.0349, 31.0299, 31.0329

7. 6.5, 6.499, 6.511

8. .1376, .1369, .1368

9. 12.82, 12.821, 12.9

___ ___ ___ ___ ___ ___ ___ ___ ___
  8   4   6   1   9   3   5   7   2

Put in increasing order.

10. 16.198, 16.199, 16.189

11. 102.09, 102.101, 102.011

12. 8.0321, 8.0322, 8.03121

13. .6032, .6132, .6022

Put in decreasing order.

14. .301, .311, .302

15. 12.1212, 12.1221, 12.1222

16. 4.404, 4.414, 4.441

17. .7811, .7812, .7821

Rounding Decimals

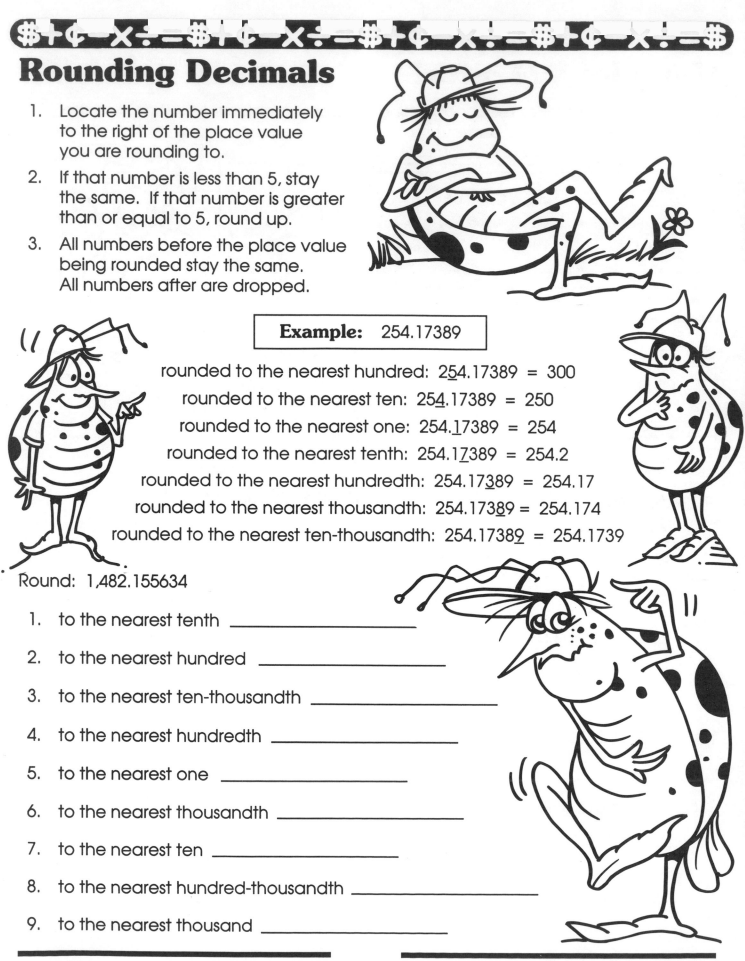

1. Locate the number immediately to the right of the place value you are rounding to.

2. If that number is less than 5, stay the same. If that number is greater than or equal to 5, round up.

3. All numbers before the place value being rounded stay the same. All numbers after are dropped.

Example: 254.17389

rounded to the nearest hundred: 254.17389 = 300

rounded to the nearest ten: 254.17389 = 250

rounded to the nearest one: 254.17389 = 254

rounded to the nearest tenth: 254.17389 = 254.2

rounded to the nearest hundredth: 254.17389 = 254.17

rounded to the nearest thousandth: 254.17389 = 254.174

rounded to the nearest ten-thousandth: 254.17389 = 254.1739

Round: 1,482.155634

1. to the nearest tenth _____

2. to the nearest hundred _____

3. to the nearest ten-thousandth _____

4. to the nearest hundredth _____

5. to the nearest one _____

6. to the nearest thousandth _____

7. to the nearest ten _____

8. to the nearest hundred-thousandth _____

9. to the nearest thousand _____

Itchy Insects

Only which mosquitoes bite? To find out, follow the directions below.

1. Put an E above number 2 if 3.596 rounded to the nearest one is 4.

2. Put an A above number 1 if 23.4512 rounded to the nearest ten is 23.

3. Put an O above number 5 if 649.3 rounded to the nearest hundred is 650.

4. Put an E above number 6 if 2.19 rounded to the nearest tenth is 2.2.

5. Put an M above number 1 if .0388 rounded to the nearest hundredth is .039.

6. Put a C above number 5 if 57.86 rounded to the nearest ten is 58.9.

7. Put a D above number 3 if 4.355 rounded to the nearest hundredth is 4.35.

8. Put an A above number 4 if 14.86 rounded to the nearest one is 15.

9. Put an L above number 5 if .2315 rounded to the nearest thousandth is .232.

10. Put a B above number 2 if 717.1717 rounded to the nearest tenth is 717.17.

11. Put an M above number 3 if 5.066 rounded to the nearest one is 5.

12. Put a D above number 6 if 44.689 rounded to the nearest ten is 44.7.

13. Put an F above number 1 if .86424 rounded to the nearest ten-thousandth is .8642.

___   ___   ___   ___   ___   ___
 1   2   3   4   5   6

Adding Decimals

Example 1		
3.498 + 2.056		3.498 + 2.056 5.554

1. Line up decimal points.
2. Add zeros to keep position if necessary.
3. Bring decimal point down.
4. Add, carrying when needed.

Example 2		
1.18 + .5782		1.1800 + .5782 1.7582

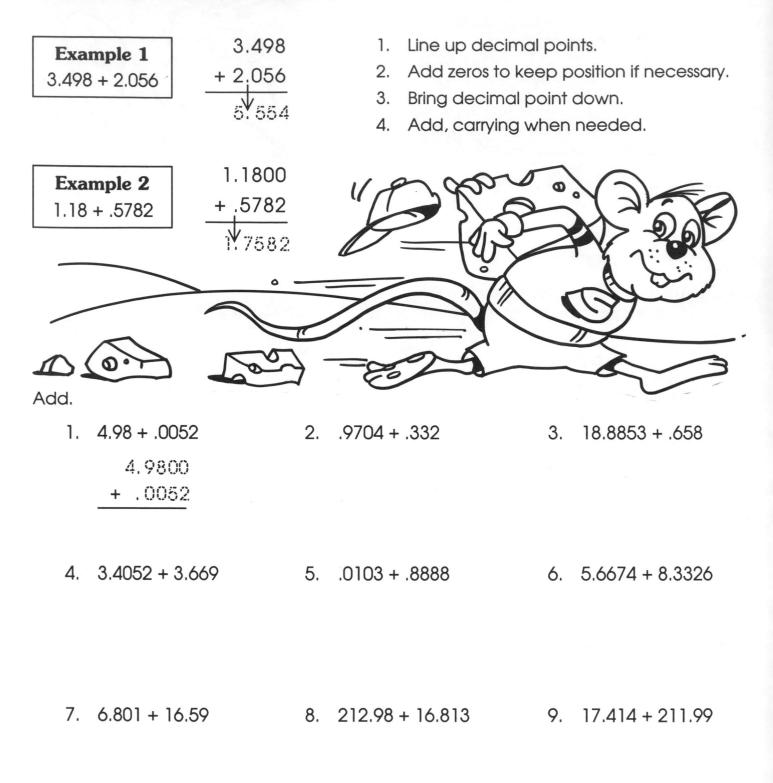

Add.

1. 4.98 + .0052

    4.9800
    + .0052

2. .9704 + .332

3. 18.8853 + .658

4. 3.4052 + 3.669

5. .0103 + .8888

6. 5.6674 + 8.3326

7. 6.801 + 16.59

8. 212.98 + 16.813

9. 17.414 + 211.99

©MCMXCIV Instructional Fair, Inc.

Swiss Sentences

Finish these cheesy number sentences.

1.862	+	.9854	=	
+		+		
.53	+	6.72	=	
=		=		
	+		=	
				+

.9076	+	.995	=	
+		+		=
6.53	+	5.47	=	
=		=		
	+		=	

Estimating Decimal Sums

When estimating decimal sums, round to whole numbers to make the addition easy. If you were at the market and had a $10 bill and wanted to buy items that cost $2.27, $4.83 and $1.95, you could estimate their sum to know if you had enough money with you.

Nearest One

$$
\begin{array}{rcr}
2.27 & \to & 2 \\
4.83 & \to & 5 \\
+\,1.95 & \to & +\,2 \\
\hline
9.05 & & 9
\end{array}
$$

Actual = 9.05
Estimated = 9
Difference = .05

Nearest Ten

$$
\begin{array}{rcr}
48.99 & \to & 50 \\
+\,22.25 & \to & +\,20 \\
\hline
71.24 & & 70
\end{array}
$$

Actual = 71.24
Estimated = 70
Difference = 1.24

Remember, look at the number to the right of the place value you are rounding to. If that number is < 5, the number you are rounding stays the same. If that number is ≥ 5, the number you are rounding goes up by 1.

Estimate.

1.
$$
\begin{array}{rcr}
3.864 & \to & 4 \\
5.27 & \to & 5 \\
+\,6.911 & \to & +\,7 \\
\hline
\end{array}
$$

2.
$$
\begin{array}{r}
33.96 \\
+\,48.13 \\
\hline
\end{array}
$$

3.
$$
\begin{array}{r}
28.034 \\
+\,74.105 \\
\hline
\end{array}
$$

4. 3.4 + 7.2 + 8.8

5. 81.6 + 52.7 + 49.8

6. 1.2 + 1.9 + 3.5

7. 79.8 + 63.9 + 82.4

8. 5.68 + 4.39 + 5.42

9. 77.41 + 63.92 + 18.88

Scoops and Cones

Draw a line from the addition problem to the estimated sum.

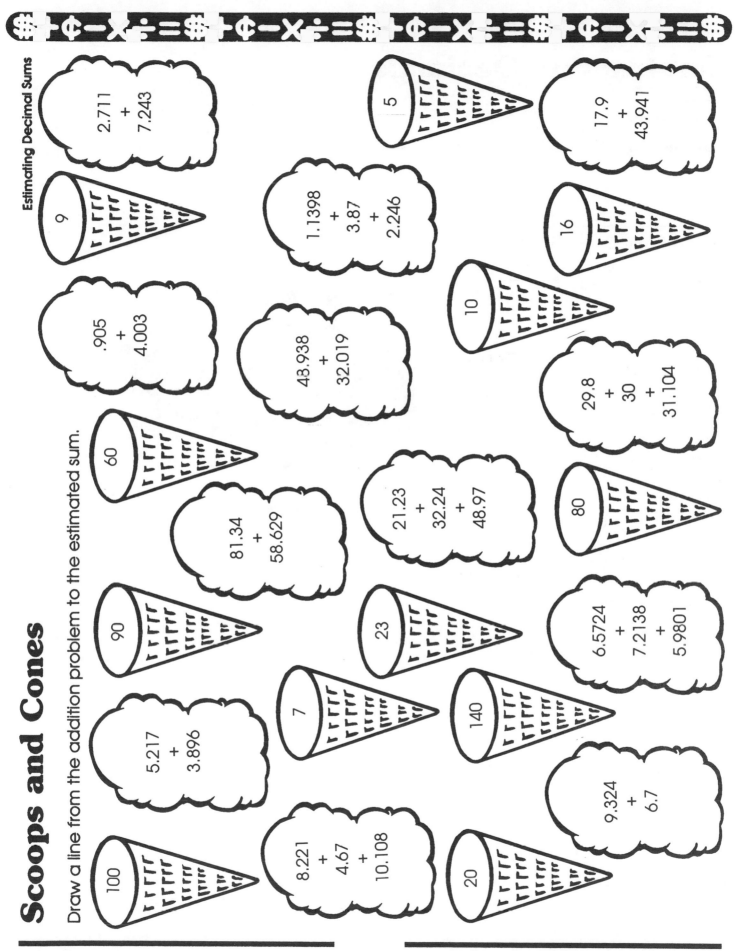

Estimating Decimal Sums

2.711 + 7.243

9

5

1.1398 + 3.87 + 2.246

17.9 + 43.941

16

.905 + 4.003

48.938 + 32.019

10

29.8 + 30 + 31.104

60

81.34 + 58.629

21.23 + 32.24 + 48.97

80

90

23

6.5724 + 7.2138 + 5.9801

5.217 + 3.896

7

140

9.324 + 6.7

100

8.221 + 4.67 + 10.108

20

Math IF5113

11

©MCMXCIV Instructional Fair, Inc.

Subtracting Decimals

Example 1
35.0469 - 14.0378

$$\begin{array}{r} 35.0469 \\ -\ 14.0378 \\ \hline 21.0091 \end{array}$$

Example 2
8.5 – 6.345

$$\begin{array}{r} 8.500 \\ -\ 6.345 \\ \hline 2.155 \end{array}$$

Example 3
13 – .54

$$\begin{array}{r} 13.00 \\ -\ \ \ .54 \\ \hline 12.46 \end{array}$$

1. Line up decimal points. With whole numbers, add a decimal point at the end.
2. Add zeros to keep position if necessary.
3. Bring decimal point down.
4. Subtract, borrowing when needed.

Subtract.

1. 3 – 2.598

$$\begin{array}{r} 3.000 \\ -\ 2.598 \\ \hline \end{array}$$

2. .8175 – .623

3. 9.86 – .0426

4. 29.586 – 14.4211

5. .8747 – .0996

6. 17 – 5.8032

7. 42.816 - 9.9123

8. 212 - 11.916

9. 21.3 - 11.815

Tut's Homework

King Tut's teacher left some subtraction problems for him to do on the wall of a pyramid. Use the following hieroglyphic decoder box to decipher the numbers. Give your answers in hieroglyphics.

1	= ★		6	= ✳
2	= ▲		7	= 🐤
3	= ❖		8	= ➡
4	= ✿		9	= ■
5	= ♥		0	= ●

★.   .✿ ▲ ❖ ➡
     − .▲ ■ ■ 🐤
_____

▲.   ♥ . ▲ ● ■
     − ✿ . 🐤 ■ ➡
_____

❖.   ★ − .● ➡ ✿
_____

✿.   ❖ . ■ ➡ ✿ ★
     − .▲ 🐤 ➡ ➡
_____

♥.   ♥ ● . ✿ ❖
     − ✿ ▲ . ★
_____

✳.   . ✳ ■ 🐤 ❖
     − .✿ ♥ ● ➡
_____

🐤.   ▲ ♥ ✿ . ■ ➡
     − ★ ➡ ✳ . ✳ ■
_____

➡. ❖ ➡ − ▲ ★ . ♥ ✿
_____

■.   ■ . ➡ 🐤
     − 🐤 . ● ✳
_____

★●.   .🐤 🐤 ✳ ➡
      − .♥ ✿ ❖
_____

★★.   ✿ ▲ . ♥ 🐤
      − ★ ❖ . ➡ ➡ ❖
_____

★▲.   ✿ ★ − ✳ . ♥ ➡ ■ ★
_____

★❖.   🐤 ❖ . ★ ➡ ➡ 🐤
     − ★ ✿ . 🐤 ● ▲ ♥
_____

★✿.   ★ ▲ ❖ . ♥ 🐤
     −   . ✳ ➡ ▲
_____

★♥.   ✳ ✳ . ● ■ ❖
     −   ➡ . ■ ■ 🐤
_____

Estimating Decimal Differences

When estimating decimal differences, round to whole numbers to make the subtraction easy to do. This comes in handy when you don't need an exact answer or when you don't have the time or the paper to do the subtraction.

Nearest One	Nearest Ten	Nearest Hundred

Nearest One:
```
  8.762  →    9
- 4.103  →  - 4
  4.659  →    5
```
Actual = 4.659
Estimated = 5
Difference = .341

Nearest Ten:
```
  63.45  →   60
- 28.86  →  - 30
  34.59       30
```
Actual = 34.59
Estimated = 30
Difference = 4.59

Nearest Hundred:
```
  339.62  →   300
-  93.99  →  - 100
  245.63       200
```
Actual = 245.63
Estimated = 200
Difference = 45.63

Remember, look at the number to the right of the place value you are rounding to. If that number is < 5, the number you are rounding stays the same. If that number is ≥ 5, the number you are rounding goes up by 1.

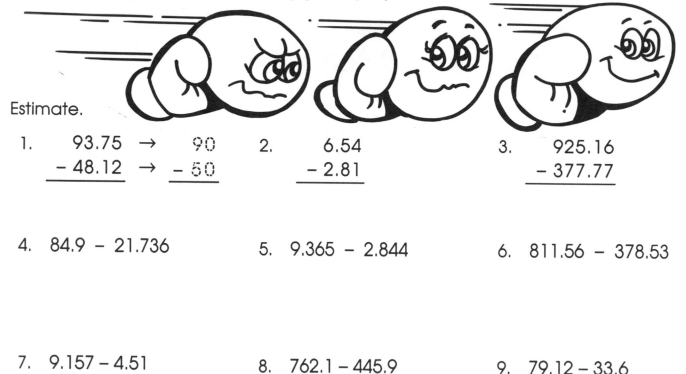

Estimate.

1.
```
  93.75  →   90
- 48.12  →  - 50
```

2.
```
  6.54
- 2.81
```

3.
```
  925.16
- 377.77
```

4. 84.9 – 21.736

5. 9.365 – 2.844

6. 811.56 – 378.53

7. 9.157 – 4.51

8. 762.1 – 445.9

9. 79.12 – 33.6

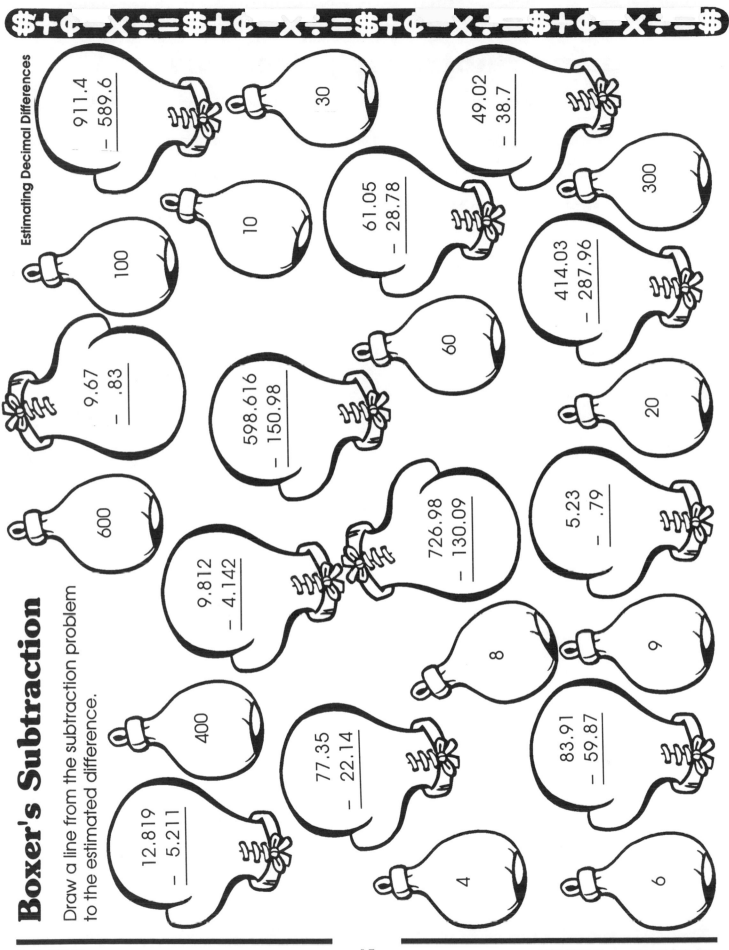

Boxer's Subtraction

Draw a line from the subtraction problem to the estimated difference.

Estimating Decimal Differences

911.4
− 589.6
_____

30

49.02
− 38.7
_____

10

61.05
− 28.78
_____

300

100

414.03
− 287.96
_____

9.67
− .83
_____

598.616
− 150.98
_____

60

20

600

9.812
− 4.142
_____

726.98
− 130.09
_____

5.23
− .79
_____

8

9

400

77.35
− 22.14
_____

83.91
− 59.87
_____

12.819
− 5.211
_____

4

6

Adding and Subtracting Decimals

Sometimes it is necessary to add and subtract many decimals. An example of this would be balancing a checkbook. There are two ways to do this.

> **Example:** 16.98 − 8.42 + 39.15 − 46.23 + 15.44 − 11.96

1. Add and subtract from left to right.

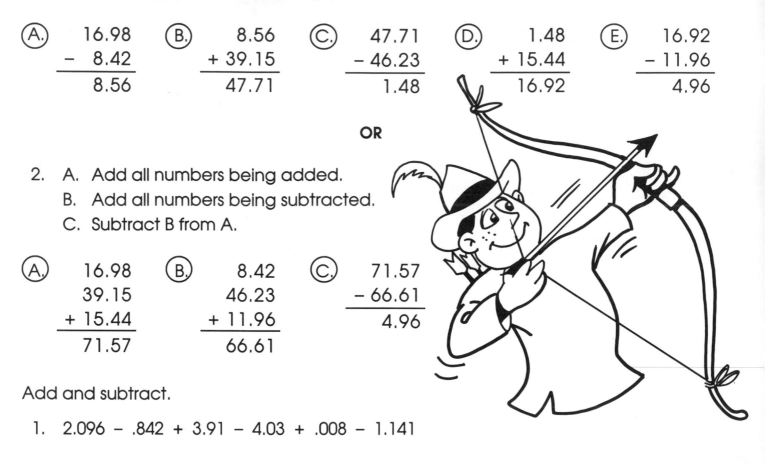

Ⓐ
$$
\begin{array}{r}
16.98 \\
-\ 8.42 \\
\hline
8.56
\end{array}
$$

Ⓑ
$$
\begin{array}{r}
8.56 \\
+\ 39.15 \\
\hline
47.71
\end{array}
$$

Ⓒ
$$
\begin{array}{r}
47.71 \\
-\ 46.23 \\
\hline
1.48
\end{array}
$$

Ⓓ
$$
\begin{array}{r}
1.48 \\
+\ 15.44 \\
\hline
16.92
\end{array}
$$

Ⓔ
$$
\begin{array}{r}
16.92 \\
-\ 11.96 \\
\hline
4.96
\end{array}
$$

OR

2. A. Add all numbers being added.
   B. Add all numbers being subtracted.
   C. Subtract B from A.

Ⓐ
$$
\begin{array}{r}
16.98 \\
39.15 \\
+\ 15.44 \\
\hline
71.57
\end{array}
$$

Ⓑ
$$
\begin{array}{r}
8.42 \\
46.23 \\
+\ 11.96 \\
\hline
66.61
\end{array}
$$

Ⓒ
$$
\begin{array}{r}
71.57 \\
-\ 66.61 \\
\hline
4.96
\end{array}
$$

Add and subtract.

1. 2.096 − .842 + 3.91 − 4.03 + .008 − 1.141

2. 143.63 − 98.74 + 65.13 − 104.39 + 71.09 − 12.82

3. 26.17 + 39.56 + 43.71 − 88.44 − 17.51 + 20.04

4. 1,596.05 − 800.96 + 3,782.75 − 312.31 + 500.04

Adding and Subtracting Decimals

Robin Hood's Loot

As you know, Robin Hood stole from the rich and gave to the poor. Follow his stealing and giving path to figure out how much he has left for himself at the end.

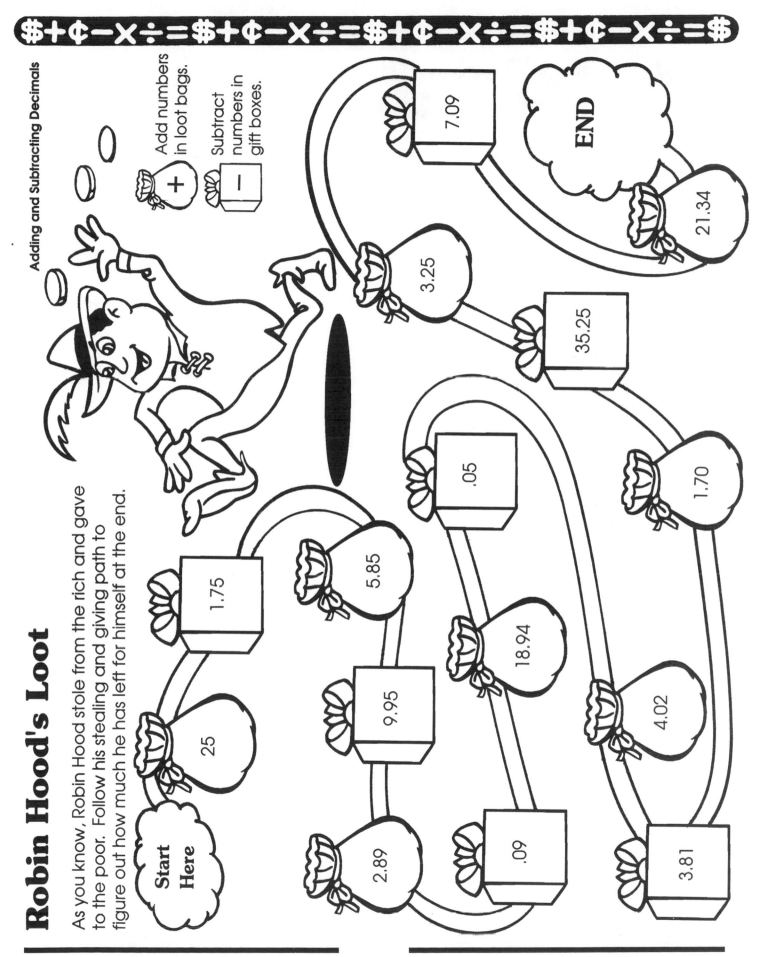

Add numbers in loot bags.

Subtract numbers in gift boxes.

Start Here

25

1.75

5.85

.05

7.09

3.25

35.25

1.70

18.94

9.95

4.02

2.89

.09

3.81

21.34

END

Multiplying Decimals
(Two-Digit Multiplier)

Example
.268 x .17

$$
\begin{array}{r}
.268 \leftarrow 3 \text{ places} \\
\times\ .17 \leftarrow 2 \text{ places} \\
\hline
1876 \\
+\ 2680 \\
\hline
.04556 \leftarrow 5 \text{ places}
\end{array}
$$

1. Put numbers in position to multiply.
2. Multiply by ones.
3. Multiply by tens. (Add zero to keep position.)
4. Add.
5. Count the number of places to the right of the decimal points.
4. Put decimal point in product the same number of places from the right. Insert zeros when necessary.

Multiply.

1.
$$
\begin{array}{r}
2.38 \\
\times\ 4.5 \\
\hline
1190 \\
+\ 9520 \\
\hline
\end{array}
$$

2.
$$
\begin{array}{r}
6.803 \\
\times\ 9.4 \\
\hline
\end{array}
$$

3.
$$
\begin{array}{r}
75.3 \\
\times\ .28 \\
\hline
\end{array}
$$

4. .438 x .11

5. 324.6 x 5.3

6. 86.1 x .49

7. 3.981 x 8.9

8. 162.9 x 3.7

9. 99.02 x .45

Major League Multiplication

What was "Babe" Ruth's real name? To find out, solve the following multiplication problems. Then, find the answers in the mitt. Put the corresponding letter above that problem's number.

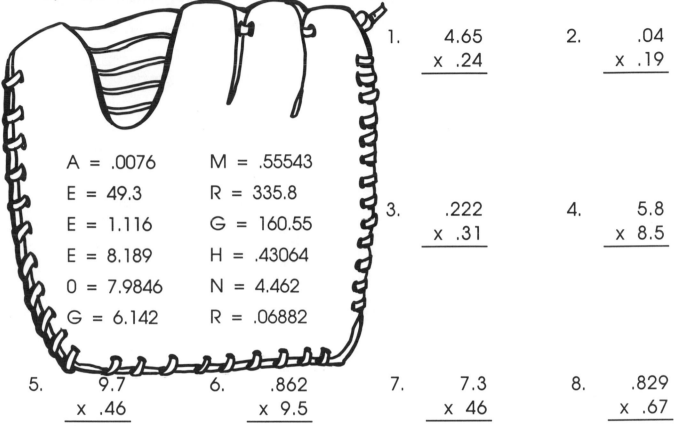

```
A = .0076      M = .55543
E = 49.3       R = 335.8
E = 1.116      G = 160.55
E = 8.189      H = .43064
O = 7.9846     N = 4.462
G = 6.142      R = .06882
```

1. 4.65
    x .24

2.   .04
    x .19

3. .222
    x .31

4. 5.8
    x 8.5

5. 9.7
    x .46

6. .862
    x 9.5

7. 7.3
    x 46

8. .829
    x .67

9. 9.62 x .83

10. .769 x .56

11. 24.7 x 6.5

12. 8.3 x .74

| 12 | 4 | 9 | 7 | 11 | 1 | | 10 | 6 | 3 | 8 | 2 | 5 |

Multiplying Decimals
(Three-Digit Multiplier)

Example	
.2187 x .306	

```
  .2187    ← 4 places
x  .306    ← 3 places
  ─────
  13122
  00000
+ 656100
  ───────
.0669222   ← 7 places
```

1. Put numbers in position to multiply.
2. Multiply by ones.
3. Multiply by tens.
4. Multiply by hundreds.
5. Add.
6. Count the number of places to the right of the decimal points.
7. Put decimal point in product the same number of places from the right. Insert zeros when necessary.

Multiply.

1.
```
      4.65
   x 78.9
   ──────
     4185
    37200
+  325500
```

2.
```
     28.8
   x 3.74
   ──────
```

3.
```
     6.033
   x  .858
   ──────
```

4. 438 x .111

5. 324.6 x 5.32

6. 86.1 x .496

7. 72.72 x 8.61

8. 4.93 x .505

9. 5.513 x 7.33

Solving for Touchdowns

Tackle this crossnumber! Decimal points
will take up their own squares.

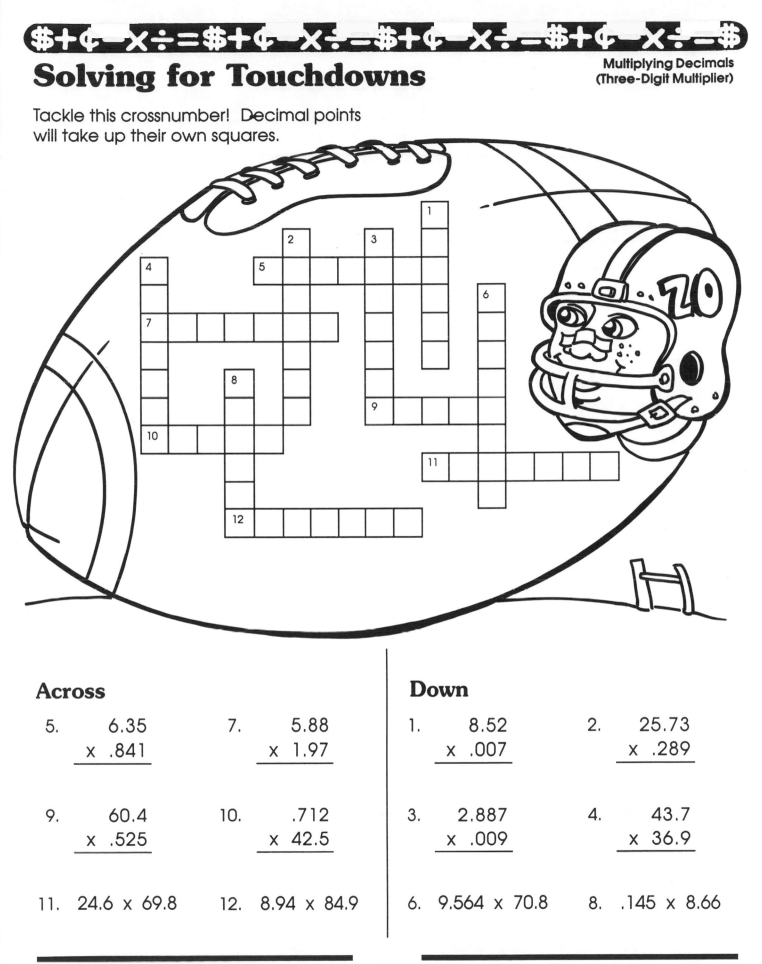

Across

5.   6.35
   x .841

7.   5.88
   x 1.97

9.   60.4
   x .525

10.   .712
    x 42.5

11. 24.6 x 69.8

12. 8.94 x 84.9

Down

1.   8.52
   x .007

2.   25.73
   x .289

3.   2.887
   x .009

4.   43.7
   x 36.9

6. 9.564 x 70.8

8. .145 x 8.66

Estimating Decimal Products

When estimating decimal products, round to a whole number to make the multiplication easy. For example, your neighbor asked you to baby-sit for 4.75 hours and pays $3.25 per hour. You'd want to figure out how much you'd earn before accepting by doing the multiplication mentally by rounding to the nearest one.

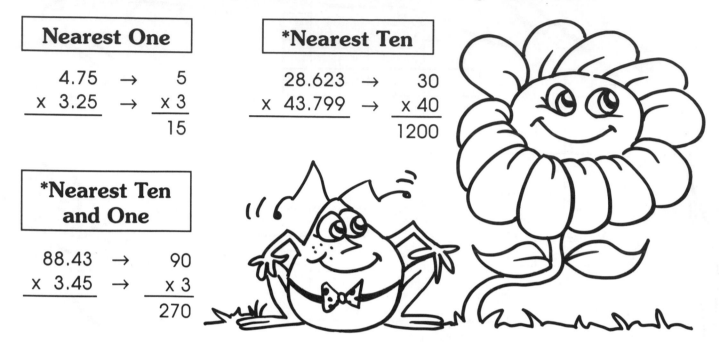

Nearest One

$$4.75 \rightarrow 5$$
$$\underline{\times\ 3.25} \rightarrow \underline{\times\ 3}$$
$$15$$

*Nearest Ten

$$28.623 \rightarrow 30$$
$$\underline{\times\ 43.799} \rightarrow \underline{\times\ 40}$$
$$1200$$

*Nearest Ten and One

$$88.43 \rightarrow 90$$
$$\underline{\times\ 3.45} \rightarrow \underline{\times\ 3}$$
$$270$$

*Multiply the non-zero numbers first. Then, count the number of zeros in the rounded numbers and add that number of zeros to the product.

Estimate.

1. $65.43 \rightarrow 70$
    $\underline{\times\ 4.59} \rightarrow \underline{\times\ 5}$

2. 2.86
    $\underline{\times\ 5.13}$

3. 33.6
    $\underline{\times\ 29.7}$

4. 93.78
    $\underline{\times\ 78.99}$

5. 8.9645
    $\underline{\times\ 5.1663}$

6. 44.04
    $\underline{\times\ 48.08}$

Planting Products

Draw a line from the multiplication problem to the estimated product.

58.114
x 63.8
_____

79.4
x 70.9
_____

2.84
x 6.16
_____

30

3,600

18.62
x 73.4
_____

33.83
x 88.7
_____

5.123
x 5.955
_____

29.42
x 5.5
_____

42.3
x 4.81
_____

18

1,400

16

81.73
x 2.8
_____

9.087
x 6.892
_____

4.24
x 3.81
_____

180

240

42.89
x 1.96
_____

5,600

63

200

2,700

80

23

Dividing Decimals by Whole Numbers

$$23 \overline{) 185.\overset{\uparrow}{6}1}$$

$$23 \overline{) 185.61}$$

$$\begin{array}{r} 8.07 \\ 23 \overline{) 185.61} \\ -184 \\ \hline 16 \\ -0 \\ \hline 161 \\ -161 \\ \hline 0 \end{array}$$

1. Bring decimal point directly up.
2. Decide where to place the first digit in the quotient.
3. Divide. Then, multiply.
   1. 185 ÷ 23 = 8
   2. 8 x 23 = 184
4. Subtract and compare.
   1. 185 – 184 = 1
   2. Is 1 less than 23? Yes.
5. Bring down. Repeat the steps.
   1. Bring down 6.
   2. 23 cannot go into 16.
   3. Bring down 1.
   4. 161 ÷ 23 = 7
   5. 7 x 23 = 161
   6. 161 – 161 = 0
6. Check.
   1. 8.07 x 23 = 185.61

Divide.

1. $$8 \overline{) 7.\overset{\uparrow 9}{3}68} \atop -72 $$

2. $$14 \overline{) .4998}$$

3. $$7 \overline{) 583.8}$$

4. $$9 \overline{) 399.78}$$

5. $$21 \overline{) 121.8}$$

6. $$6 \overline{) 438.06}$$

Decimal Trivia

What is pictured on the back of a $5 bill? To find out, solve the following division problems. Then, find the answers in the $5 bill. Put the corresponding letter above that problem's number.

A = 6.402   L = 98.04
E = .006   L = 43.25
I = 58.3   L = 2.005
I = .884   M = 7.42
O = 3.68   M = .078
O = 33.33   N = .061
C = .084   N = 60.7
        R = 1.09

1. $12\overline{)44.16}$

2. $8\overline{).624}$

3. $5\overline{)37.1}$

4. $13\overline{)11.492}$

5. $9\overline{)389.25}$

6. $6\overline{)349.8}$

7. $7\overline{)686.28}$

8. $15\overline{).09}$

9. $22\overline{)1335.4}$

10. $10\overline{)20.05}$

11. $5\overline{)166.65}$

12. $7\overline{).427}$

13. $12\overline{)76.824}$

14. $9\overline{).756}$

15. $13\overline{)14.17}$

___ ___ ___ ___ ___ ___ ___
10   4   9   14   1   7   12

___ ___ ___ ___ ___ ___ ___ ___
3   8   2   11   15   6   13   5

Dividing Decimals (One-Digit Divisor)

Example 1
4.842 ÷ .6

$$
\begin{array}{r}
8.07 \\
.6\overline{\smash{)}4.8\overset{\uparrow}{1}42} \\
-48 \\
\hline
4 \\
-0 \\
\hline
42 \\
-42 \\
\hline
0
\end{array}
$$

1. Put numbers in position to divide.
2. Move decimal in divisor to the right of number.
3. Move decimal in dividend the same number of places to the right.
4. Bring decimal point directly up to quotient.
5. Divide, adding zeros to dividend when necessary.
6. Check by multiplying.

Example 2
294 ÷ .7

$$
\begin{array}{r}
420. \\
.7\overline{\smash{)}294.0\overset{\uparrow}{}} \\
-28 \\
\hline
14 \\
-14 \\
\hline
00
\end{array}
$$

Example 3
3.18 ÷ .4

$$
\begin{array}{r}
7.95 \\
.4\overline{\smash{)}3.1\overset{\uparrow}{1}80} \\
-28 \\
\hline
38 \\
-36 \\
\hline
20 \\
-20 \\
\hline
0
\end{array}
$$

Divide.

1.
$$
\begin{array}{r}
.6 \\
.8\overline{\smash{)}.4984} \\
-48 \\
\hline
\end{array}
$$

2. $.6\overline{\smash{)}522}$

3. $.9\overline{\smash{)}5.067}$

4. 2.64 ÷ .5

5. 520.8 ÷ .7

6. 39.04 ÷ .4

Sammie Snail's Shell

Solve the following division problems. Connect the correct answers to assist Sammie Snail in getting into his shell. Write the correct answers to the problems that are wrong.

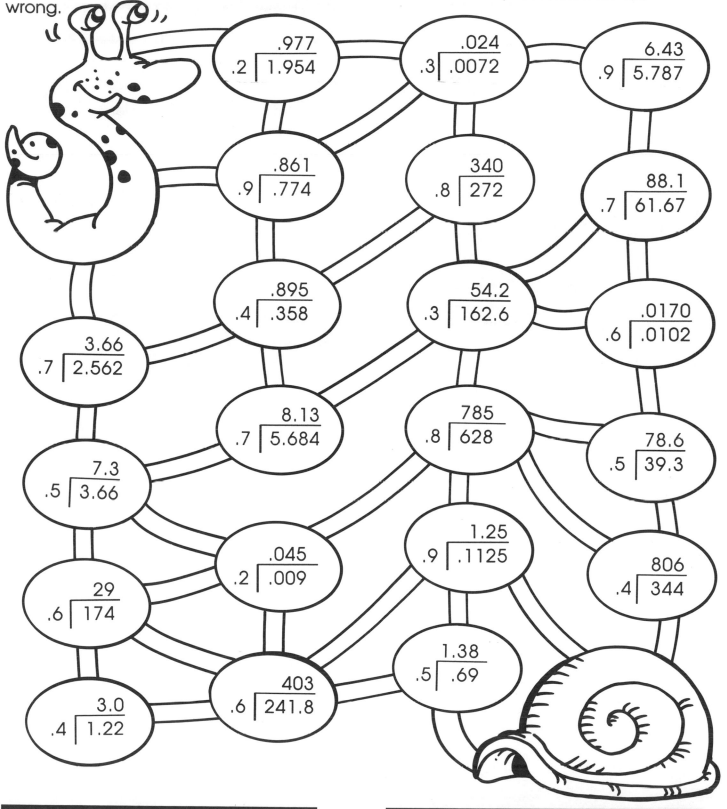

27

Dividing Decimals (Two-Digit Divisor)

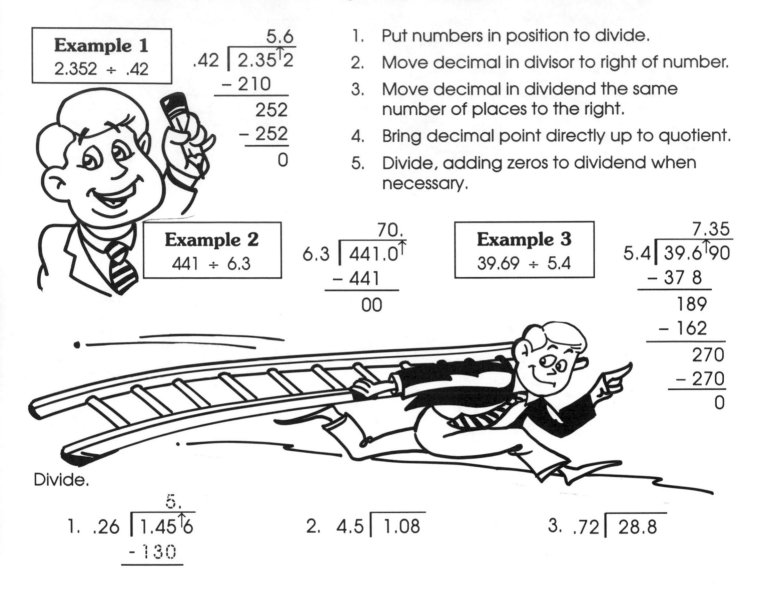

Example 1
2.352 ÷ .42

$$\begin{array}{r} 5.6 \\ .42\overline{)2.35\!\uparrow\!2} \\ -210 \\ \hline 252 \\ -252 \\ \hline 0 \end{array}$$

1. Put numbers in position to divide.
2. Move decimal in divisor to right of number.
3. Move decimal in dividend the same number of places to the right.
4. Bring decimal point directly up to quotient.
5. Divide, adding zeros to dividend when necessary.

Example 2
441 ÷ 6.3

$$\begin{array}{r} 70. \\ 6.3\overline{)441.0\!\uparrow} \\ -441 \\ \hline 00 \end{array}$$

Example 3
39.69 ÷ 5.4

$$\begin{array}{r} 7.35 \\ 5.4\overline{)39.6\!\uparrow\!90} \\ -37\;8 \\ \hline 189 \\ -162 \\ \hline 270 \\ -270 \\ \hline 0 \end{array}$$

Divide.

1. $.26\overline{)1.45\!\uparrow\!6}$ $\begin{array}{r}5.\\ -130\end{array}$

2. $4.5\overline{)1.08}$

3. $.72\overline{)28.8}$

4. 8.46 ÷ 1.8

5. 18.944 ÷ 3.7

6. 7.531 ÷ .34

Dividing Decimals (Two-Digit Divisor)

Bob Means Business

Does businessman Bob make it up the corporate ladder? Solve the following division problems and shade in the answers on the ladder to find out. If any numbers are not shaded when all the problems have been completed, Bob gets fired. Some answers may not be on the ladder.

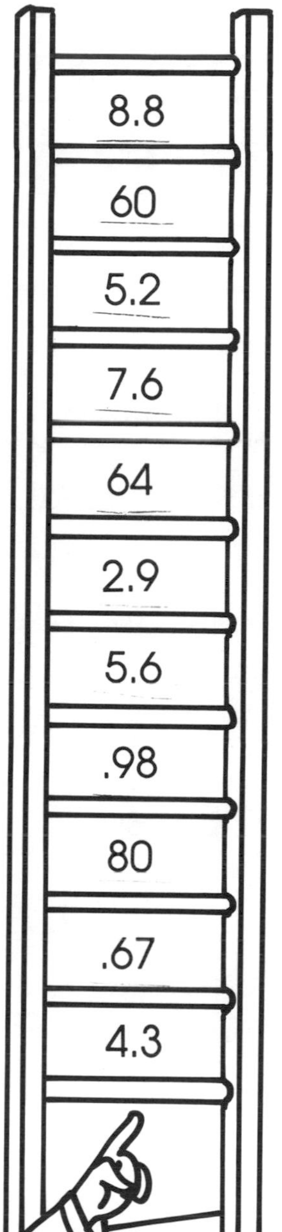
8.8
60
5.2
7.6
64
2.9
5.6
.98
80
.67
4.3

1. $.42 \overline{)3.192}$
2. $1.5 \overline{)1.47}$
3. $.22 \overline{)1.936}$
4. $3.6 \overline{)216}$
5. $.53 \overline{).3551}$
6. $.34 \overline{)1.462}$
7. $360 \div 4.5$
8. $.522 \div .18$
9. $2.325 \div 2.5$
10. $1.976 \div .38$
11. $40.32 \div .63$
12. $6.6 \div 1.2$

Does Bob make it or get fired? ______________

Estimating Decimal Quotients

When estimating decimal quotients, round to a whole number to make the division easy. For example, if you had 17.8 milliliters of medicine left and took 3.12 milliliters each day, how many days of medicine would you have left?

| **Example A** |

$17.8 \div 3.12 \rightarrow 18 \div 3 = 6$

1. Round the numbers at a place value that makes the division easy.
2. Divide the rounded non-zero numbers.
3. Cancel all zeros in the divisor and the same number of zeros in the dividend.
4. Bring up any remaining zeros.

| **Example B** |

$629.48 \div 88.23 \rightarrow 630 \div 90$

$$90\overline{)630} = 7$$

| **Example C** |

$4,489.56 \div 52.6 \rightarrow 4,500 \div 50$

$$50\overline{)4500} = 90$$

Estimate.

1. $14.97 \div 2.73$

$$3\overline{)15}$$

2. $476.92 \div 62.8$

3. $3,589.662 \div 88.74$

4. $36.43 \div 5.782$

5. $419.551 \div 72.21$

6. $6,389.75 \div 78.57$

Put Your Best Foot Forward!

Draw a line from the division problem
to the estimated quotient.

717.5 ÷ 82.3

4

25.2 ÷ 4.8

9

31.91 ÷ 4.24

604.87 ÷ 18.5

1,756.82 ÷ 32.4

243.97 ÷ 58.7

6

3

8

17.87 ÷ 3.34

30

80

157.2 ÷ 2.3

60

198.4 ÷ 5.16

12.24 ÷ 3.9

5

40

3,492.98 ÷ 72.3

50

Multiplying and Dividing Decimals by Powers of 10

Multiplying by Powers of 10

$$1 \times .33 = .33$$
$$10 \times .33 = 3.3$$
$$100 \times .33 = 33$$
$$1{,}000 \times .33 = 330$$

To multiply a decimal by a power of ten, move the decimal point one place to the right for each zero in the power of ten.

Dividing by Powers of 10

$$28.6 \div 1 = 28.6$$
$$28.6 \div 10 = 2.86$$
$$28.6 \div 100 = .286$$
$$28.6 \div 1{,}000 = .0286$$

To divide a decimal by a power of ten, move the decimal point one place to the left for each zero in the power of ten.

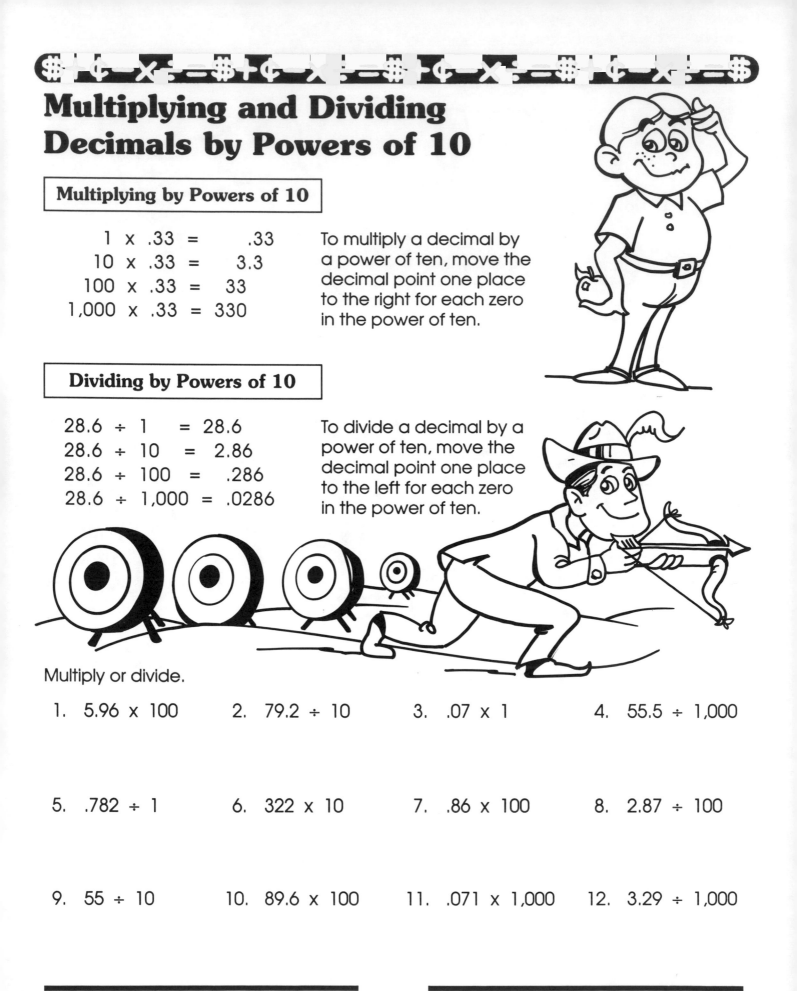

Multiply or divide.

1. 5.96 x 100

2. 79.2 ÷ 10

3. .07 x 1

4. 55.5 ÷ 1,000

5. .782 ÷ 1

6. 322 x 10

7. .86 x 100

8. 2.87 ÷ 100

9. 55 ÷ 10

10. 89.6 x 100

11. .071 x 1,000

12. 3.29 ÷ 1,000

$+¢−×÷=$+¢−×÷=$+¢−×÷=$+¢−×÷=$

Wheels of Wonder

**Multiplying and Dividing
Decimals by Powers of 10**

Find each product or quotient. Multiply or divide each number by the number in the center.

Wheel 1: x 10 — 7.76, .92, 87, .88, 5.5
Wheel 2: ÷ 100 — 8.98, 29.8, 21, .32, 5.6
Wheel 3: ÷ 10 — 6.72, 5.19, 39, 52.5, .08
Wheel 4: x 1,000 — 49.8, 10.9, .77, .099, 3.22
Wheel 5: x 100 — 5.51, 872, 91, .072, 6.6
Wheel 6: ÷ 1,000 — 7.32, 54.12, .93, 21.2, 81

Math IF5113

33

©MCMXCIV Instructional Fair, Inc.

Writing Decimals as Percents and Percents as Decimals

Decimals as Percents

To write a decimal as a percent, move the decimal point 2 places to the right and add a % sign. You may need to insert zeros.

.50 = .50 = 50%

.62 = .62 = 62%

1.4 = 1.40 = 140%

.07 = .07 = 7%

Percents as Decimals

To write a percent as a decimal, move the decimal point 2 places to the left and omit the % sign. You may need to insert zeros.

63% = 63 = .63

90% = 90 = .9

1% = 01 = .01

.2% = 00.2 = .002

Write as a percent.

1. .39   2. .08   3. 1.2   4. .6

5. 7   6. 2.01   7. .002   8. 5.67

Write as a decimal.

9. 78%   10. 50%   11. 9%   12. 3.3%

13. .01%   14. 7%   15. 60.2%   16. .009%

Happy Anniversary!

When did the Statue of Liberty celebrate its 100th anniversary? Shade in the true equations to get the answer.

.06 = 6%	30% = 3.0	301% = 3.01	89% = .89	.4 = 40%	6.2% = .62	.51 = 51%	84% = .84	17% = .17	.87 = 8.7%	185% = 1.85	.9 = 9%	4.8% = .48
72% = .72	.6 = 6%	.006 = .6%	.5 = 5%	5% = .05	.63 = 6.3%	7% = .07	1.6 = 16%	.11 = 11%	2.9% = .29	.09 = 9%	40% = .04	.77 = 7.7%
1.5 = 150%	.1% = .01	.43 = 43%	8% = .08	3.6 = 360%	34% = 3.4	160% = 1.6	.06 = 6%	222% = 2.22	10.1 = 101%	90% = .9	4.29 = 42.9%	87% = .087
.2% = .002	5.4 = 54%	65% = 6.5	1.5 = 15%	69% = .69	7% = .7	.37 = 37%	93% = 9.3	1.9 = 190%	64% = 6.4	.001 = .1%	12% = .12	65% = .65
4% = .04	4.8% = .48	.13 = 1.3%	104% = 10.4	.23 = 23%	313% = .313	2% = .02	3.8 = 38%	30% = .3	.13 = 1.3%	1% = .01	55.5 = 555%	38% = .38
.99 = 99%	830% = .83	.6 = 6%	98% = 9.8	.9% = .009	.625 = 625%	.004 = 4%	.8 = 80%	92% = .92	.02 = 20%	4.4% = .044	.55 = 55%	.2 = 20%

Writing Fractions as Percents and Percents as Fractions

Fractions as Percents

$$\frac{3}{8} = $$

$$\begin{array}{r} .375 \\ 8\overline{\smash)3.000} \\ -24 \\ \hline 60 \\ -56 \\ \hline 40 \\ -40 \\ \hline 0 \end{array}$$

1. Divide numerator by denominator.
2. Write this decimal as a percent.

$$.375 = 37.5\%$$

Percents as Fractions

$$55\% = .55$$

fifty-five hundredths $= \frac{55}{100}$

$$\frac{55}{100} \begin{array}{c} (\div 5) \\ (\div 5) \end{array} = \frac{11}{20}$$

1. Write percent as a decimal.
2. Write decimal as a fraction using the place value.
3. Reduce by dividing numerator and denominator by the greatest common factor (GCF).

Write as a percent.

1. $\frac{3}{4}$

2. $\frac{2}{25}$

3. $\frac{3}{10}$

4. $\frac{1}{2}$

5. $\frac{2}{5}$

6. $\frac{7}{8}$

7. $\frac{1}{4}$

8. $\frac{7}{10}$

Write as a reduced fraction.

9. 60%

10. 25%

11. 44%

12. 5%

13. 32%

14. 64%

15. 76%

16. 18%

36

Incredible Inventions

What did Samuel Benedict invent? Find out by solving the following problems and finding the answers in the test tube. Put the corresponding letter above that problem's number at the bottom of the page.

Write as a percent.

1. $\frac{1}{4}$

2. $\frac{5}{8}$

3. $\frac{7}{10}$

4. $\frac{13}{100}$

5. $\frac{3}{5}$

6. $\frac{7}{20}$

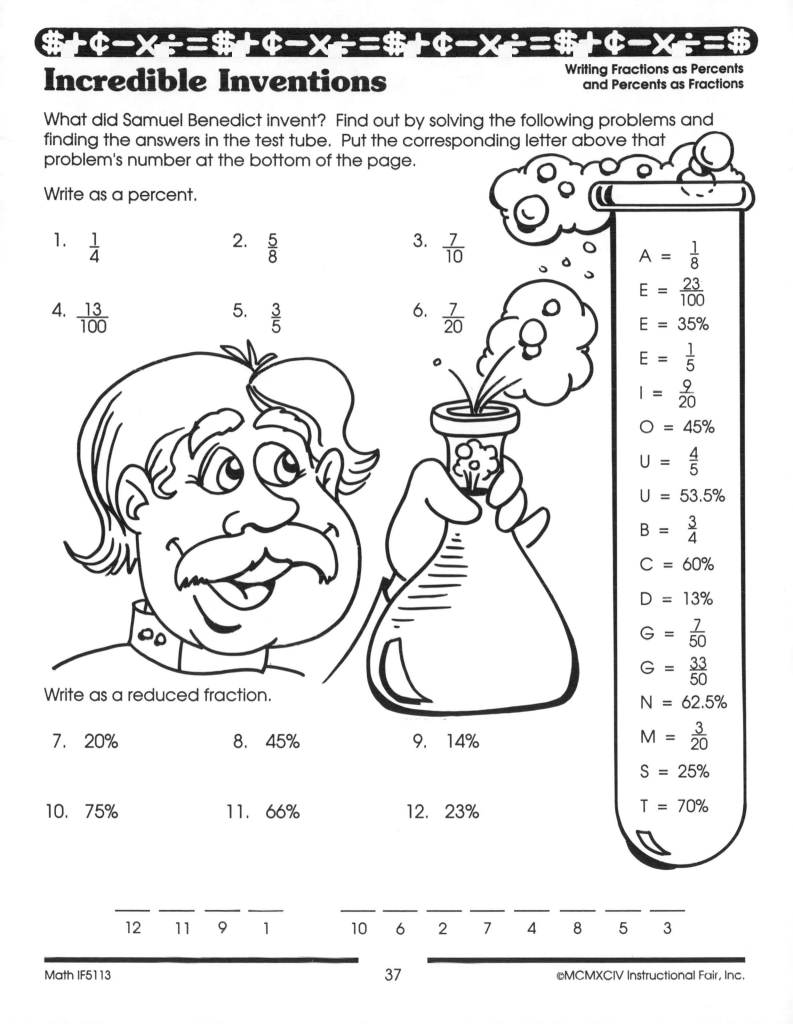

A = $\frac{1}{8}$

E = $\frac{23}{100}$

E = 35%

E = $\frac{1}{5}$

I = $\frac{9}{20}$

O = 45%

U = $\frac{4}{5}$

U = 53.5%

B = $\frac{3}{4}$

C = 60%

D = 13%

G = $\frac{7}{50}$

G = $\frac{33}{50}$

N = 62.5%

M = $\frac{3}{20}$

S = 25%

T = 70%

Write as a reduced fraction.

7. 20%

8. 45%

9. 14%

10. 75%

11. 66%

12. 23%

___ ___ ___ ___   ___ ___ ___ ___ ___ ___ ___ ___
12   11   9   1   10   6   2   7   4   8   5   3

Decimals, Fractions and Percents

	Decimal	Percent	Fraction
Example 1 .45	.45	.45 = 45%	forty-five hundredths $\dfrac{45}{100}\dfrac{(\div 5)}{(\div 5)} = \dfrac{9}{20}$
Example 2 61%	61% = .61	61%	sixty-one hundredths $\dfrac{61}{100}$
Example 3 $\dfrac{11}{20}$	$20\overline{)11.00}$ $.55$ -100 100 -100 0	.55 = 55%	$\dfrac{11}{20}$

Write as a percent.

1. .205

2. $\dfrac{3}{100}$

3. 1.8

4. $\dfrac{9}{50}$

5. .43

6. $\dfrac{4}{5}$

Write as a decimal.

7. 4.6%

8. $\dfrac{4}{5}$

9. 125%

10. $\dfrac{9}{10}$

11. 99%

12. $\dfrac{7}{8}$

Write as a reduced fraction.

13. .12

14. 90%

15. .06

16. 4%

17. .36

18. 35%

38

Mirthful Mugs

Put the correct eyes and mouth on the faces by finding the decimal and reduced fraction for each percent.

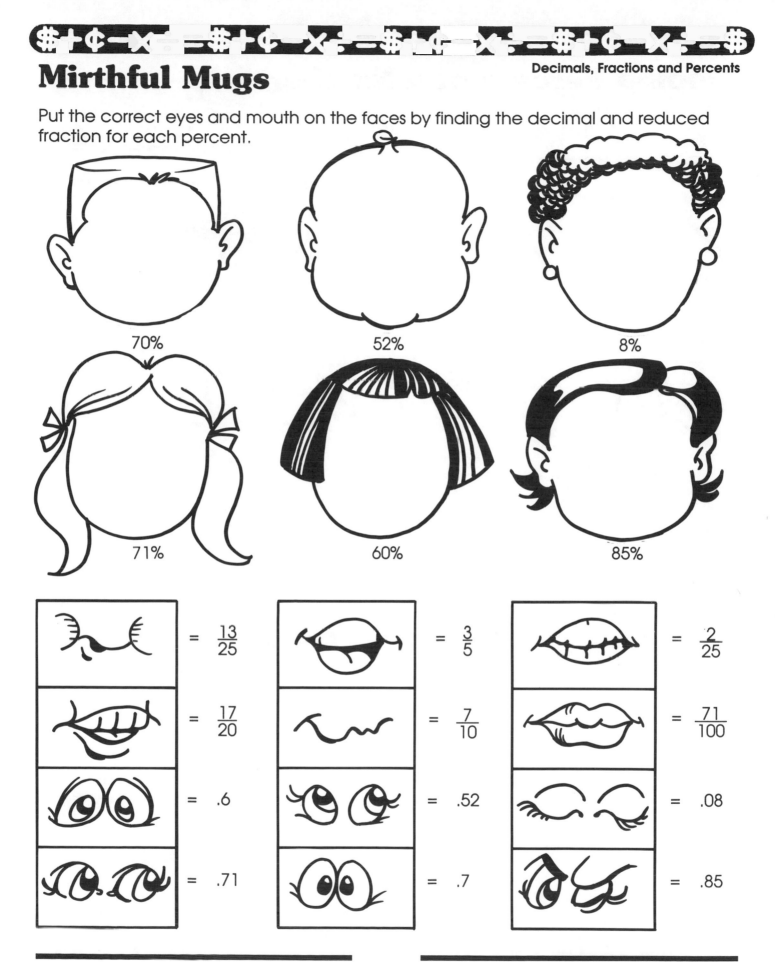

70%

52%

8%

71%

60%

85%

$= \dfrac{13}{25}$

$= \dfrac{3}{5}$

$= \dfrac{2}{25}$

$= \dfrac{17}{20}$

$= \dfrac{7}{10}$

$= \dfrac{71}{100}$

$= .6$

$= .52$

$= .08$

$= .71$

$= .7$

$= .85$

Finding Percent of a Number

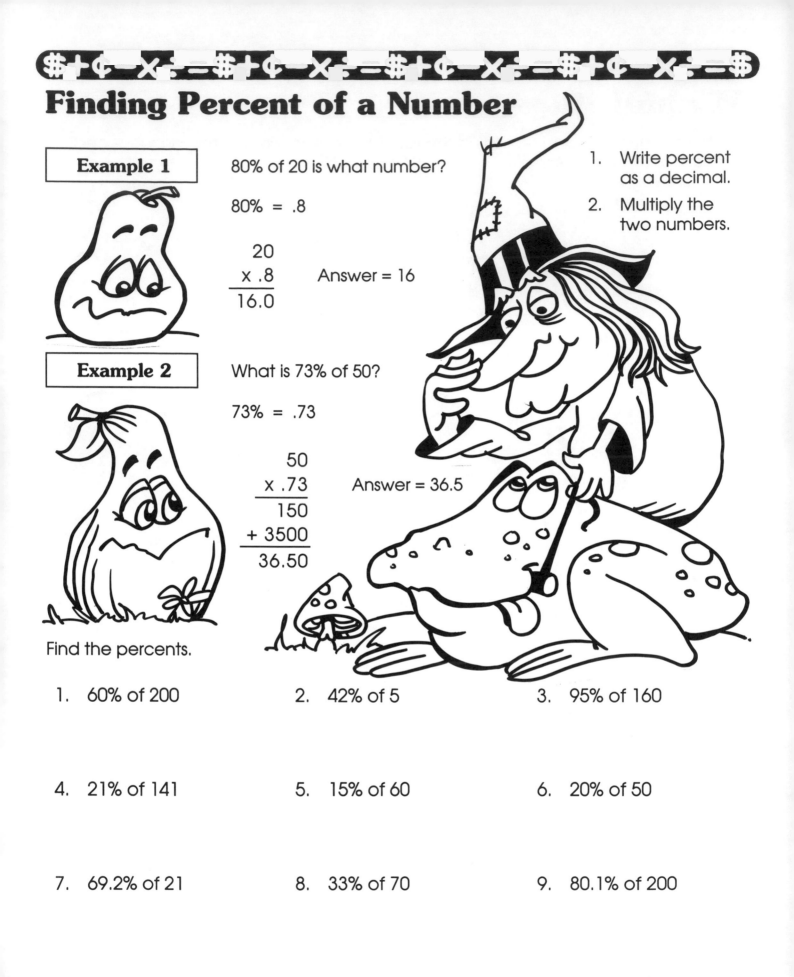

Example 1

80% of 20 is what number?

80% = .8

```
   20
 x .8        Answer = 16
 16.0
```

1. Write percent as a decimal.
2. Multiply the two numbers.

Example 2

What is 73% of 50?

73% = .73

```
     50
   x .73      Answer = 36.5
    150
 + 3500
  36.50
```

Find the percents.

1. 60% of 200

2. 42% of 5

3. 95% of 160

4. 21% of 141

5. 15% of 60

6. 20% of 50

7. 69.2% of 21

8. 33% of 70

9. 80.1% of 200

Wacky Wanda's Wecipe

Wacky Wanda the Witch alters her family recipe for goulash to suit her taste. Figure out the new amounts Wanda needs for her delicious goulash and put the letters above the answers at the bottom of the page.

❃ Gross Goulash ❃

Stir together:

40 worms

70 strands of hair

24 snails

150 toenails

150 rutabagas

600 ants

120 cat whiskers

80 teeth

200 cloves of garlic

40 roaches

Simmer for 6 days.

Wanda likes:

A. 5% of the teeth

E. 62% of the cloves of garlic

I. 150% of the snails

O. 125% of the cat whiskers

B. 30% of the worms

N. 108% of the ants

P. 90% of the toenails

P. 15% of the roaches

T. 20% of the hair

T. 2% of the rutabagas

12	150	648

4	6	135	124	14	36	3

41

Sales and Discounts

SPRING·FLING·SALE!

Sale Prices

$88.75 20% off

100%	= full price
− 20%	= discount
80%	= you pay

80% = .8

```
  88.75
x   .8
71.000
```
↓
$71 is the
sale price.

```
  88.75
x   .2
17.750
```
↘
$17.75 is the savings.

OR

```
  88.75
− 71.00
  17.75
```
↙

HUGE SALE!!!

Discounts

Paul the produce peddler gives a 10% discount if you pay your bill within 7 days.
Your bill was $212.50, and you paid on the 4th day. What did you pay?

10% = .1

You pay Paul:

```
$212.50
x    .1
$21.250
```
↓
$21.25 is the
discount.

```
$212.50
x    .9
$191.250
```
↘
$191.25

OR

```
$212.50
−  21.25
$191.25
```
↙

What is the sale price of a $62 sweater if it is:

1. 30% off   2. 25% off   3. 15% off   4. 80% off

What is your discount if your bill is $49.50 and you get a:

5. 10% discount   6. 30% discount   7. 4% discount   8. 50% discount

Bobby's Bargain Bonanza

Bargain Betty loves to get a good deal and won't buy anything unless it's on sale. So, she decided to go to Bobby's Bargain Basement where everything is on sale.

★ Bobby's Bargain Basement ★

skirts	$26.50 → 40% off		sweaters	$32.40 → 20% off
shirts	$24.00 → 25% off		jeans	$18.50 → 10% off
shoes	$28.60 → 15% off		boots	$30.00 → 12% off
socks	$7.20 → 35% off		dresses	$31.90 → 50% off
pants	$27.40 → 30% off		belts	$12.00 → 8% off
coats	$34.00 → 45% off		robes	$28.20 → 5% off

Answer the following questions using Bobby's price list and find the answers at the bottom of the page. Put that problem's letter above the answer to find a word describing Betty. See if your parents know this word!

A. What is the discount on shoes?

I. What is the sale price for a pair of socks?

I. What is the sale price for a pair of pants?

O. What is the discount on shirts?

O. What is the discount on coats?

U. What is the sale price for a skirt?

M. What is the discount on boots?

N. What is the sale price for a robe?

P. What is the sale price for a sweater?

R. What is the discount on jeans?

S. What is the sale price for a belt?

S. What is the discount on dresses?

___ ___ ___ ___ ___ ___   ___ ___ ___ ___ ___ ___

$25.92 $4.29 $1.85 $11.04 $19.18 $3.60 $6.00 $26.79 $4.68 $15.30 $15.90 $15.95

43

ANSWER KEY

Decimals and Percents

Grade 6

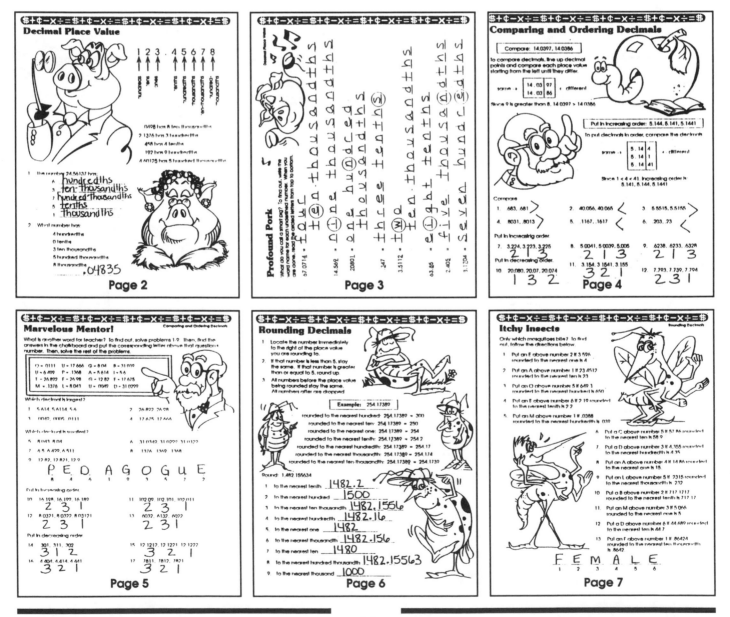

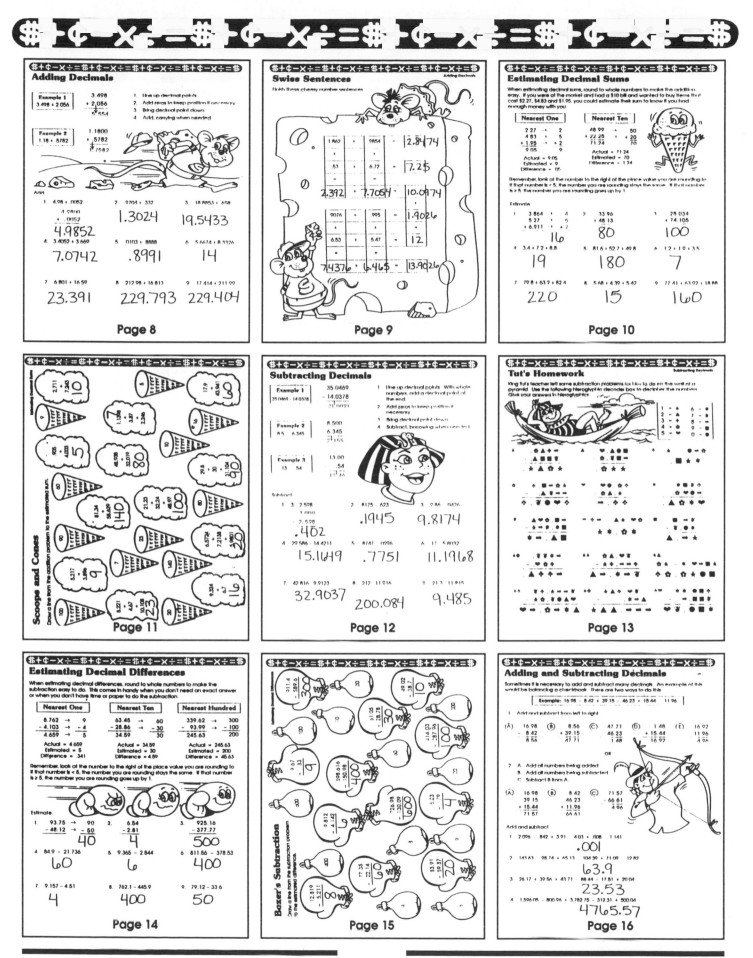

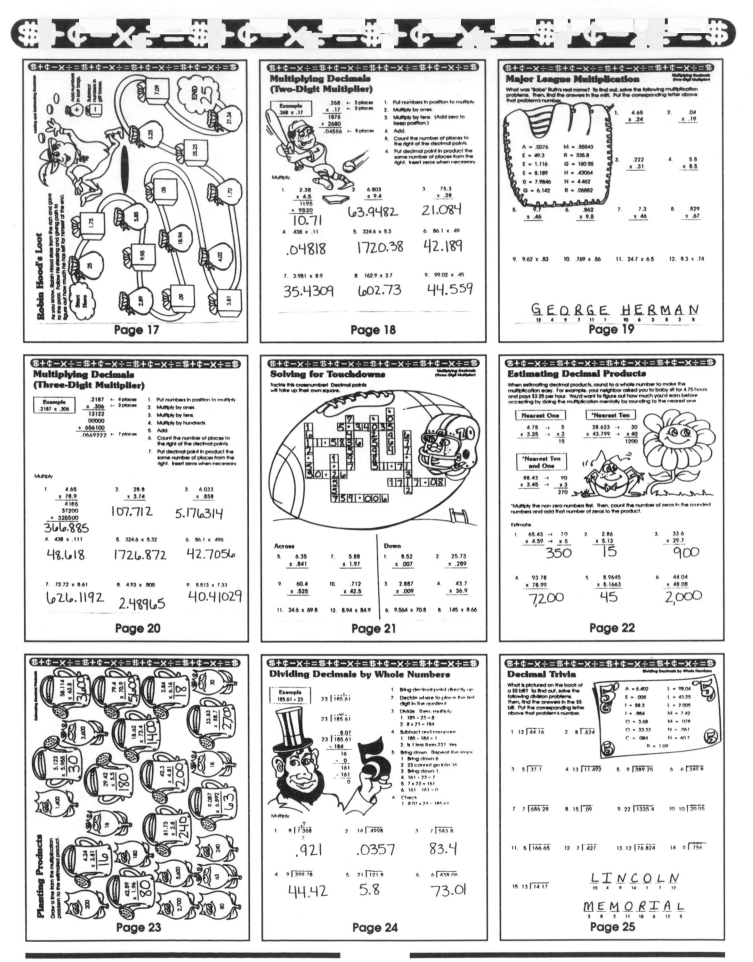

Page 17 — Robin Hood's Loot

END 25

7.09, 21.34, 3.25, 35.25, .05, 1.70, 1.75, 5.65, 18.94, 4.02, 9.98, .25, 2.89, .09, 3.81

Page 18 — Multiplying Decimals (Two-Digit Multiplier)

Example: .268 × .17

1. 2.38 × 4.5	2. 6.803 × 9.4	3. 75.3
10.71	63.9482	21.084

4. 438 × .11	5. 324.6 × 5.3	6. 86.1 × 49
.04818	1720.38	42.189

7. 3.981 × 8.9	8. 162.9 × 3.7	9. 99.02 × .45
35.4309	602.73	44.559

Page 19 — Major League Multiplication

A = .0076   M = .55643
E = 49.3   R = 335.8
E = 1.116   G = 160.55
E = 8.189   H = .43064
O = 7.9846   N = 4.462
G = 6.142   R = .06882

G E O R G E   H E R M A N
12 4 7 11 1 10   6 3 8 2 5

Page 20 — Multiplying Decimals (Three-Digit Multiplier)

Example: .2187 × .306

1. 4.65 × 78.9	2. 28.8 × 3.74	3. 6.033 × .858
366.885	107.712	5.176314

4. 438 × .111	5. 324.6 × 5.32	6. 86.1 × .496
48.618	1726.872	42.7056

7. 72.72 × 8.61	8. 4.93 × 505	9. 5.513 × 7.33
626.1192	2.48965	40.41029

Page 21 — Solving for Touchdowns

Across
5. 6.35 × .841   7. 5.88 × 1.97
9. 60.4 × .525   10. .712 × 42.5
11. 24.6 × 69.8   12. 8.94 × 84.9

Down
1. 8.52 × .007   2. 25.73 × .289
3. 2.887 × .009   4. 43.7 × 36.9
6. 9.564 × 70.8   8. .145 × 8.66

Page 22 — Estimating Decimal Products

1. 65.43 × 4.59	2. 2.86 × 5.13	3. 33.6 × 29.7
350	15	900

4. 93.78 × 78.99	5. 8.9645 × 5.1663	6. 44.04 × 48.08
7,200	45	2,000

Page 23 — Planting Products

3,600; 5,600; 18; 3,000; 2,700; 30; 18; 200; 1,400; 63; 16; 160; 240; 80; 2,700; 80; 240; 63

Page 24 — Dividing Decimals by Whole Numbers

Example: 185.61 ÷ 23

1. 8) 7.368	2. 14) 4998	3. 7) 583.8
.921	.0357	83.4

4. 9) 399.78	5. 21) 121.8	6. 6) 438.06
44.42	5.8	73.01

Page 25 — Decimal Trivia

A = 6.402   L = 98.04
E = .005   E = 43.25
I = 58.3   L = 2.005
I = .884   M = 7.42
O = 3.68   M = .078
O = 33.33   N = 60.7
C = .084
R = 1.09

L I N C O L N
10 4 9 14 1 7 2

M E M O R I A L
3 8 2 11 18 6 13 5

Page 23, Page 24, Page 25

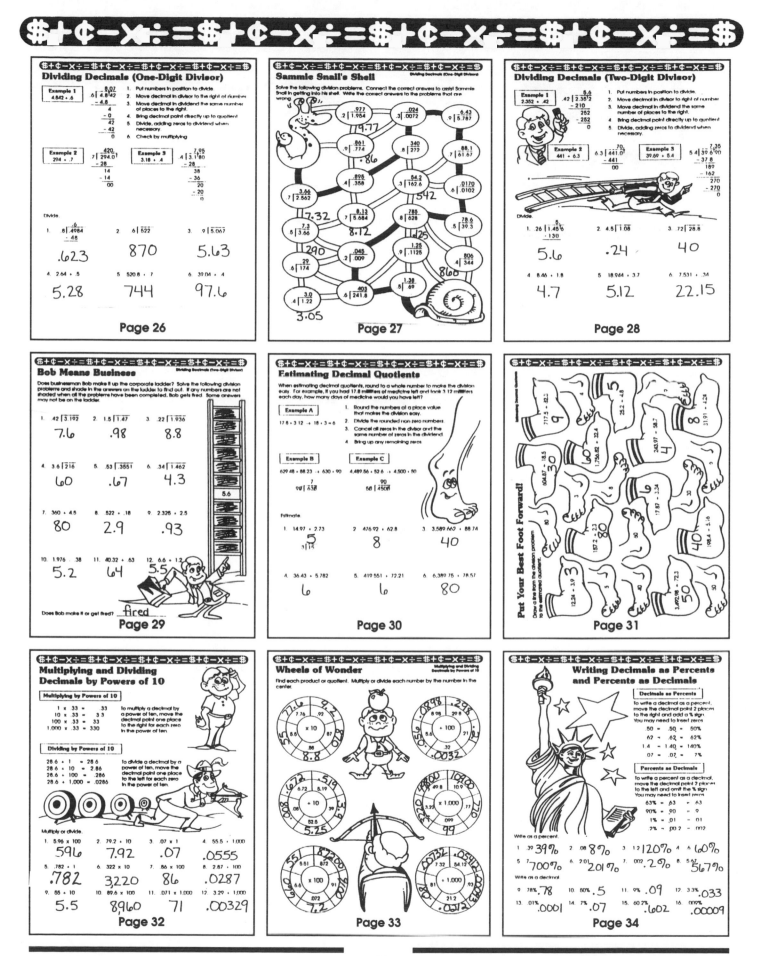

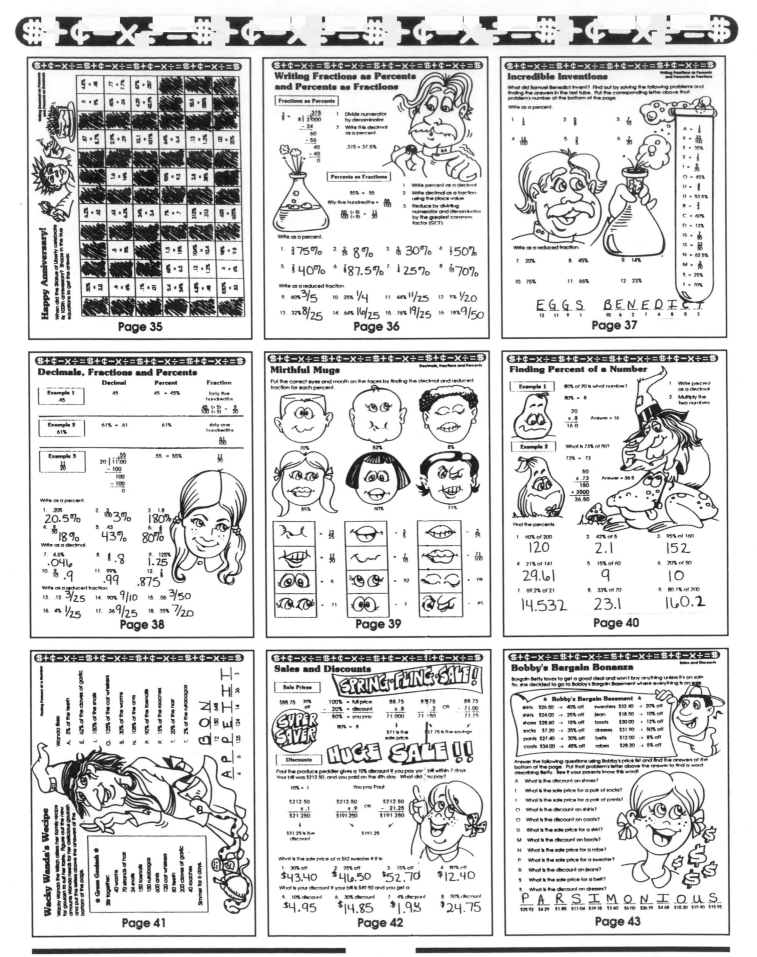

Page 35 — Happy Anniversary!

Page 36 — Writing Fractions as Percents and Percents as Fractions

Write as a percent.
1. 75% 2. 8% 3. 30% 4. 50%
5. 40% 6. 87.5% 7. 25% 8. 70%

Write as a reduced fraction.
9. 3/5 10. 1/4 11. 11/25 12. 1/20
13. 8/25 14. 16/25 15. 19/25 16. 9/50

Page 37 — Incredible Inventions

EGGS BENEDICT

Page 38 — Decimals, Fractions and Percents

Write as a percent.
1. 20.5% 2. 3% 3. 180%
4. 18% 5. 43% 6. 80%

Write as a decimal.
7. .046 8. 1.8 9. 1.25
10. .9 11. .99 12. .875

Write as a reduced fraction.
13. 3/25 14. 9/10 15. 3/50
16. 1/25 17. 9/25 18. 7/20

Page 39 — Mirthful Mugs

Page 40 — Finding Percent of a Number

Find the percents.
1. 120 2. 2.1 3. 152
4. 29.61 5. 9 6. 10
7. 14.532 8. 23.1 9. 160.2

Page 41 — Wacky Wanda's Wecipe

BON APPETIT

Page 42 — Sales and Discounts

1. $43.40 2. $46.50 3. $52.70 4. $12.40
5. $4.95 6. $14.85 7. $1.98 8. $24.75

Page 43 — Bobby's Bargain Bonanza

PARSIMONIOUS